Explore the Outdoors

Trail Riding

Have Fun, Be Smart

by Allison Stark Draper

The Rosen Publishing Group, Inc.
New York

Published in 2000 by The Rosen Publishing Group, Inc.
29 East 21st Street, New York, NY 10010

First Edition

Draper, Allison Stark.
    Trail riding : have fun, be smart / Allison Draper.
        p. cm. — (Explore the outdoors)
    Includes bibliographical references and index.
    Summary: Traces the history of the horse, describes various breeds, explains how to prepare horses for the trail, and points out possible dangers when riding.
    ISBN 0-8239-3170-6
    1. Trail riding—Juvenile literature. [1. Western riding. 2. Horses.] I. Title. II. Series.
SF309.28 .D725 2000
798.2'3—dc21   99-049768
                                                                    CIP
                                                                    AC

Manufactured in the United States of America

Contents

Introduction

Trail riding is the purest way to spend time with your horse. It is waking at dawn to meander on horseback through fields of Maine mist. It is whispering your horse up the slick granite of Colorado mountain passes. It is cantering through the splattering foam of a New Jersey beach. It is galloping at sunset across the California desert. It can also be a slow walk through a suburban neighborhood or a bracing trot around the reservoir in New York City's Central Park. To trail ride is simply to ride away from stable and corral, drinking in the scenery and being at one with your horse.

Trail riding is a favorite pastime of many horseback riders. Not only in the United States but all over the world, trail riding is the way most recreational riders spend the most time with their horses. There are two main styles of riding in America: Western and English. In England, trail riding is called "hacking" and descends from the woodland travels of adventuring knights and the wild cross-country rides of fox hunters. Western trail riding traces back to the cattle ranchers and cowboys of the western plains, the legendary horsemanship of the American Indians, and the undying allure of the wide open frontier of the Wild West.

In this book you will learn how to become involved in trail riding. You will learn about the different breeds of horses and how to groom and take care of a horse. You will learn the basic skills of riding and how to stay safe on horseback. As a teen, you will discover a new and exciting activity that combines love of the wilderness and open spaces with a unique bond to another living creature, and you will experience a form of travel that is thousands of years old.

Horses and their riders will bond together.

1 The History of the Horse

The horse is at least 50 million years old. A fossil of the earliest known horse ancestor (Hyracotherium) was found in North America. The size of a large dog, it had four toes on its front feet and three on its hind feet and lived in forests and swamps. As changes in the earth's climate produced grassy, open plains, the early horse became faster. Its legs grew longer, and it lost one of the four toes on its front feet. About ten to fifteen million years ago, a grazing version of the modern horse appeared.

These ancient cave paintings in Lascaux, France, indicate that humans have appreciated the horse for thousands of years.

The "true," or one-toed, horse (Equus) that we know today probably originated in North and Central America. At one time, Alaska and Russia were still connected by a land bridge. Some of these original horses crossed this land bridge into Asia and traveled across to Europe and down into Africa. Horses then became extinct on the American continents but thrived in Europe, Asia, and Africa. Equus is therefore the source of all modern horses all over the world. It is also the source of such horse relatives as the donkey and the zebra.

Humans have been riding horses for almost five thousand years. Historically, horses have provided people with transportation, companionship, meat, and milk. They have carried hunters after large and fast game. They have carried warriors into battle. They have also represented material wealth. In times when money was not in common use, owning horses showed that a person was rich and important.

Cave paintings from the Stone Age suggest that very early peoples used a harness or collar to control their horses. The hunters who stalked wild horse herds for meat discovered that horses could be tamed. Some of these nomadic peoples traveled great distances with their horses. They introduced the use of horses to people they met and allowed their horses to interbreed with wild horses during their journeys. By 3000 BC, both the nomadic peoples of Asiatic Russia and the peoples of ancient Assyria and Babylonia were keeping horses, riding horses, and using horses to pull and carry heavy loads.

One important early use of the horse was in war. The Egyptians used horses to pull their weapon-filled chariots into battle. The Persians, who were excellent riders, rode into battle and found horses to be a great advantage. A mounted warrior

This ancient sculpture shows a Hittite warrior charging into battle with his chariot horse.

is both taller and more agile than a charioteer. By 500 BC, the Persians had developed cavalry squadrons of horses powerful enough to carry riders wearing heavy armor. The ancient Greeks were also strong riders and fought on horseback like their mythical centaurs.

The Romans used hundreds of thousands of horses in their armies. They also used horses in the construction of their temples, monuments, and roads. They brought horses from southern to northern Europe and far to the east. They

Wild horses

are responsible for the interbreeding that created such breeds as the Dale and Fell ponies of England.

In the eighth century, the Moors invaded Europe. They brought thousands of Barb and Arabian horses into Spain. In the sixteenth century, the Spanish invaded America and brought their Spanish Barbs across the Atlantic Ocean by ship. Millions of years after its journey across the Alaskan land bridge, the horse had finally returned to its birthplace in North America.

The American Horse

The history of the American frontier is all about courage and stamina. The Western horse, who has both, had a lot to do with building the West. Bred to handle cattle, the Western horse is fast enough to outrun a wild bull and enduring enough to gallop all day long carrying a two-hundred-pound man and one hundred pounds of rope. It is nimble enough to stop dead from a gallop and strong enough to throw its weight against that of an uncooperative cow. It is smart and brave enough to herd or help lasso a steer. A cow horse also has to be reliable and obedient because on foot a cowboy has no protection from the long horns of wild cattle.

The early Californian cattle ranchers imported Spanish horses called Barbs. The Barb breed is known for its spirit and endurance. Barbs came originally from the Barbary region of North Africa and were used widely on the Spanish plains, both areas of the world that resemble parts of the American West.

The Barb is the traditional horse of the Bedouin nomads of the North African deserts. Barbs were brought to Spain by the Moors, and there the breed mixed with the native Spanish horses to create the Spanish Barb. Usually bay (reddish brown with a black mane and tail), brown, chestnut, black, or gray, the Barb stands fourteen to fifteen hands high, which means 4'8" or 5' at the shoulder. A "hand" is four inches, or the width of the average human palm. Typically, the Barb has a long, straight head; large, forward-set eyes; a strong, erect neck; a short, compact body; a low-set tail; and long, sleek legs. It is courageous, quick-tempered, sure-footed, and very tough.

Some of the Barbs the ranchers brought to America escaped and ran wild on the North American plains. Their offspring adapted to the tough conditions of the plains and became the wild Mustangs of the West. These horses were adopted by the Native American tribes of the plains. When English-speaking settlers arrived in the West, they discovered that Mustangs were ideal for

American horses come in many colors, such as bay, gray, and Appaloosa.

cattle ranching. A strong Mustang could carry its rider eighty to one hundred miles in a day.

The American horse was born in all colors. Spotted Appaloosas, two-toned Pintos, and silver-maned golden Palominos are all American breeds descended from the original Mustangs. Today, Western horses fall into three main categories: the dependable trail horse, the nimble ranch horse, and the beautiful show horse. Many Western horses have some Quarter Horse blood. Quarter Horses trace their lineage back to early crossbreeding between the tough Spanish cow horse and the faster, more elegant English Thoroughbred. Known as "America's horse," the Quarter Horse is a major competitor in such Western events as racing and rodeo.

2 Choosing a Horse

If you are lucky enough to be looking for your very own horse, look carefully. Keep in mind your particular needs and the reasons why you want a horse. Every horse is different in its skills, strengths, and temperament. A horse will not be right for you simply because you fall in love with it. When you choose the right horse and ride it on trails or competitive courses, you will love its ability to support you

Your horse is your friend.

and become your close working partner on the trail.

It is important to learn as much as possible when you are looking for a horse. You should meet and talk to a wide range of experienced riders, breeders, trainers, and veterinarians. You may want to ask for guidance from a riding instructor or a 4-H leader who knows your strengths and weaknesses as a rider.

You should think about temperament as well as ability. Perhaps you want to start with a pony. Maybe you want a jumper. Perhaps you want a docile, gentle horse, or a horse that will be comfortable on dry or rocky terrain. Whatever you decide, you must like a horse's personality. The breed characteristics that affect personality are a good starting point for your search.

The Breeds

An important thing to consider when choosing a horse is what breed you think matches your needs. Like dogs, who have many breeds with different qualities, there is amazing variety in horse breeds. What makes a breed distinctive? Well, some ancient

Horses and Ponies

If you know a little about the horse world, you might know that, in general, horses are big and ponies are little. What you may not know is that ponies do not grow up to be horses.

A pony compared to a horse is like a terrier compared to a German shepherd. Ponies are not baby horses, but fully grown, pint-sized breeds of the species of modern horses, Equus!

The word for baby horse is "foal." If a foal is a boy, he is a colt, and if she is a girl, she is a filly.

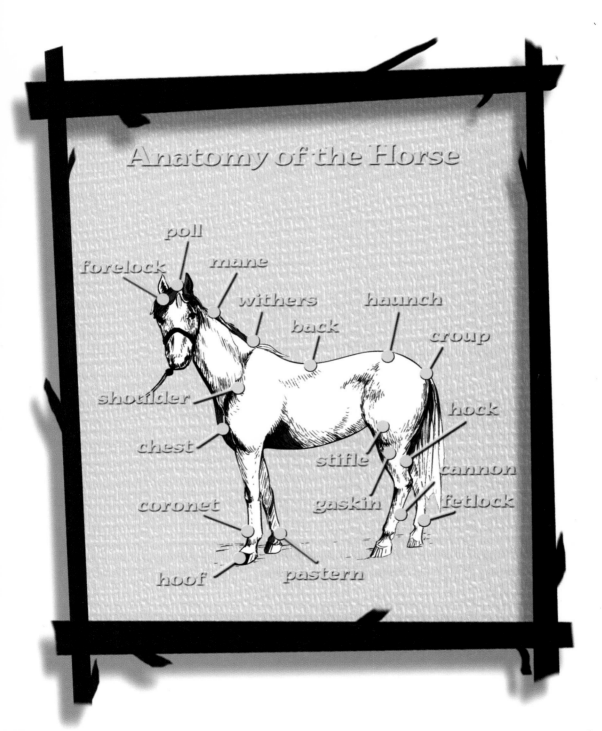

Anatomy of the Horse

poll
forelock
mane
withers
haunch
back
croup
shoulder
hock
chest
stifle
cannon
coronet
gaskin
fetlock
hoof
pastern

14

breeds, like the Arabian, were bred for their beauty, intelligence, and endurance. Other breeds, like the huge Clydesdales (which you might recognize as the horses in the Budweiser commercials) were bred for their great strength. Then there are breeds that look unique, such as Appaloosas, which are special because of their spotted markings. Read on to learn about just a few of the many breeds of horses there are in the world.

The Shetland Pony

Named for its homeland, the Shetland Islands of northern Scotland, the Shetland pony is one of the smallest horses in the world. It is also one of the strongest for its size. In the 1800s, this combination of strength and small size made it

very useful as a workhorse in the coal mines. Its size also makes it a good pony for young riders. It is lively and smart and performs well in shows and competitions. Shetlands do tend to have minds of their own, so their riders need to be confident and assertive. Otherwise, a Shetland pony can be headstrong and hard to control.

Shetland pony

The tiny Shetland is only about 10.2 hands, or 3' 6" at the shoulder. It is usually brown, black, bay, chestnut, gray, or two-colored. It has a small head, a compact, thickset body, and short legs with "feathers," or tufts of hair, on them.

The Welsh Pony

The original Welsh Mountain Pony is an ancient breed. It existed as long ago as the Roman invasion of England. After thousands of years in the craggy Welsh mountains, the Welsh pony is surefooted and quick, as well as a good jumper. It is also brave, gentle, and intelligent. Welsh ponies are excellent for both beginners and experienced riders.

The modern Welsh pony is considered one of the prettiest ponies and owes its beautiful dished face to the fact that it has some Arabian blood.

Welsh ponies

Welsh ponies come in most colors. They are not higher than twelve hands, or four feet, at the shoulder. They have small heads, high-set tails, and elegant short legs.

The Arabian

The Arabian is the oldest purebred horse in the world. There are eight-thousand-year-old rock paintings of horses in northern Africa that look like today's Arabian. The most famous Arabians are those of the Bedouin Arabs. The ancient Bedouins needed horses that could survive in their hot, dry desert homeland. They also wanted horses beautiful enough to demonstrate their wealth and power. For more than two

The Arabian horse

thousand years, they have bred their bravest and strongest mares with their most intelligent and beautiful stallions. They are very careful never to breed one of their horses with a horse whose blood is not pure Arabian.

When an Arabian does breed with another horse, its offspring always have some Arabian qualities, such as stamina, high-spiritedness, and shape. This makes the Arabian a very popular breeding horse. It has been crossed with almost every other kind of horse in the world. The Arabian is also a good riding horse. It is a particularly good horse for trail riding because of its endurance. The Arabian is usually chestnut, bay, or gray. It stands between fourteen and fifteen hands, or around five feet at the shoulder. It has a small head with a dished face and large, wide-set eyes; an arched neck; short back; and long, finely boned legs.

The Mustang

The Mustang is the wild horse of North America. As we have said, it is the descendant of the Spanish settlers' horses and has both Barb and Arabian blood. In the three hundred years that Mustangs ran wild on the western plains, they evolved into tough, smart, independent horses. Many of the best Mustangs were caught by American Indians and later by cowboys and used as riding horses.

The Mustang was crossed with larger breeds to produce larger workhorses for pulling wagons and stagecoaches. Eventually, it was crossed with the Thoroughbred. The offspring of the Mustang and the Thoroughbred is one of the most important American breeds, the Quarter Horse. There is also Mustang blood in Appaloosas, Palominos, and Pintos. There are not many

This Mustang has Appaloosa markings.

wild Mustangs left. Today they are considered endangered and are protected by law.

Mustangs come in all colors. They stand fourteen to fifteen hands, or around five feet high, at the shoulder. They are lightweight with strong legs. They are nimble and hardy and can be headstrong. Today they are used as ranch horses and for recreational and endurance riding.

The Thoroughbred

The Thoroughbred is the world's racehorse. It is the fastest horse in the world. It is also the most valuable. Developed in the 1700s, the Thoroughbred is the child of the fastest British mares and Arabian, Barb, and Turk stallions. All serious racing Thoroughbreds are the descendants of three Arabian stallions: the Byerley Turk, the Darley Arabian—the great-grandfather of Eclipse, one of the most famous racehorses of all time—and the Godolphin Arabian.

The Thoroughbred comes in most solid colors and stands tall at 14.2 to 17.2 hands, or around 5' 6," at the shoulder. It has an elegant head, a long arched neck, long back, long legs, a deep chest, and muscular hindquarters. It is bold and spirited but not headstrong or stubborn. It has a long, smooth stride and is a perfect riding horse.

The Thoroughbred horse

Colors and Markings

Horses come in a wide range of colors and markings. Like many animals, horses were originally the same color as their environments and therefore less visible to predators. This is called camouflage. Many early horses were dun, which is a yellow-gray color that made them hard to see on grassy plains. Today most horse colors have to do with breeding and human desires.

The color of a horse is the color of its coat. Its markings are its points (mane, tail, and lower legs) and face. Common horse colors include black, bay (reddish brown or red with black points), liver chestnut (brown), chestnut (red), gray, palomino (gold with white points), and paint or pinto (two-colored). Common facial markings include stripes, stars, and blazes.

star

stripe

blaze

3 Getting to Know Your Horse

Horses have unique personalities, just like people.

When you do find a horse you think you like, inspect it carefully. Note its good and bad qualities. Even a horse you really love will probably have some bad qualities.

See if you seem to fit together well with the horse when you ride around the ring. Get a sense of the horse's personality. Think about your own personality. Ask yourself whether you want a gentle horse. Ask yourself if you will be able to handle a horse with a bold or quick temper. Always remember that at some point your life may depend upon your horse's reliability and intelligence.

People are often skeptical of the idea that horses are intelligent creatures with definite personalities. There is no question that horses think. Just like people, some of them are smarter than others. In fact, some horses are clever enough to make your life impossible. There are horses who can figure out how to let themselves out of any stall, stable, barn, or paddock. There are horses who will figure this out, wait until you aren't paying attention, and let out not only themselves but all of their stablemates.

As animals in the wild, horses are herd members. They depend upon the leadership and intelligence of a dominant member, usually a stallion, to make survival decisions. There are numerous legends about wild herds that were able to avoid capture by

Don't underestimate your horse's intelligence.

4 Grooming, Tacking Up, and Dressing to Ride

A proper bridle makes your horse more comfortable.

Now that you have found your horse companion—whether your very own or a temporary friend at a school or stable—you have to learn to take care of her. When you plan to ride, you will need to have your horse groomed and tacked, that is, saddled and bridled.

Give your horse some time to digest after she has been watered and fed. Then slide a halter over her head, hook it to a lead rope, and lead her into the barn or barnyard to groom her. Start with a hard plastic curry comb. Use quick circular motions along her neck and body to loosen the dirt and dead hair from her hide. Always move from ears to

Be gentle and soothing when grooming a horse.

tail and never touch the delicate skin of a horse's face or legs with anything more than a cloth or soft brush. After currying, take a stiff hard brush and whisk out the dirt, again from front to back. Then take a soft brush and smooth down her coat and legs. Comb out her mane and tail with a wide-toothed metal comb and then go over them with the soft brush.

After grooming, you will need to check your horse's feet. Stand shoulder to shoulder with her, facing her tail, and run your hand slowly and firmly down the inside of her leg. When you reach her ankle, slide your hand around her pastern (the part of the foot between the hoof and the fetlock) and press tailward until she lifts her hoof. Horses are extremely touchy about their feet, and with good reason. In the center of the foot is a tender triangle of flesh called the frog that is easily irritated by stones, splinters, or careless humans. Once you have her hoof in your hand, support it firmly. Take a hoof pick and use a gentle front to back motion along the inside of her shoe to scrape out any dirt, stones, or horse manure that may have collected there. Be very careful not to scrape the frog.

Tacking Up

Now your horse is groomed and ready to be tacked up. Lead her to a clear area of the barn so that you can move around her easily and tie her lead rope to a hook or fence rail. When you tack up your horse, make sure you are using equipment that fits her. The saddle pad and girth (the band that encircles the horse's waist) press directly against your horse's skin, muscle, and bone. If something rubs her, the pressure will not only be painful, it may also lower her level of trust in you. If she associates pain or discomfort with being ridden by you, she will respond less enthusiastically to your demands. Horses who have bad experiences with tacking can become difficult to saddle. They may nip, kick, buck, or run away.

A modern saddle

The Saddle

To avoid aggravating your horse, check that the tree (frame) of your saddle conforms to the curve of her spine. A saddle is designed so that its tree spreads your weight over your horse's muscular back and lifts the weight off her sensitive spine. The tree needs to match the angle of her back. A saddle with a narrow tree will pinch a wide-backed horse. A wide tree will press on the withers (the ridge between the shoulders) of a narrow horse. The tree should ride clear of the withers; otherwise it may cause saddle sores. With your full weight in the saddle, you should be able to fit three fingers between your pommel (the knob at the front of the saddle) and your horse's withers.

The saddle rests on a saddle pad of heavy felt that absorbs sweat and keeps moisture away from your horse's back. A saddle pad will protect your horse's skin from the leather of your saddle, but it will not compensate for a poorly fitted saddle. When you are saddling your horse, stand on her near (left) side. Be sure that she is able to see

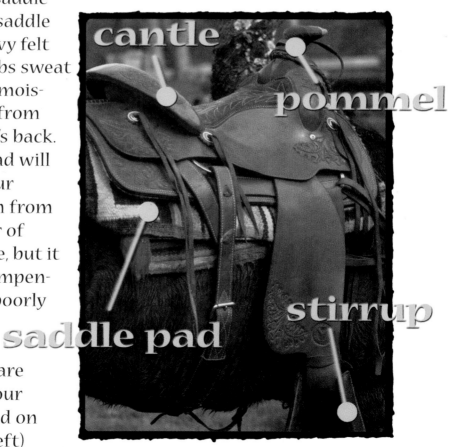

cantle

pommel

saddle pad

stirrup

you at all times. Talk soothingly to her and tell her what you are doing. Like most of us, horses are most irritable—and most likely to bite or kick—when they are not sure what is happening.

Put your left hand on the pommel (front) and your right hand on the cantle (back) of the saddle and lift it with both hands. Make sure that the off (right) stirrup is lying over the top of the saddle so that it doesn't hit her side when you set it down on her back. Place the saddle in the concavity of her back so that it doesn't press on her withers or ride up onto her hindquarters. Settle it firmly into place and make absolutely sure that her hair is smoothed front to back

Proper seating of the saddle ensures your horse's comfort.

beneath it. If her hair is not smooth, she will be uncomfortable and may develop saddle sores.

Your saddle is only as secure as the girth or cinch that holds it in place. Made of canvas, mohair, or more recently of high-tech neoprene, a girth needs to be both strong and comfortable against your horse's skin. When you have the saddle on, the girth will be hanging from the edge of your saddle on your horse's off (right) side. Crouch down on her near side (and run your hand down her foreleg while you do this so that she knows where you are), then reach beneath her and grab the end of the girth. Buckle it between the back of the forelegs and the swell of her belly.

You should be able to slip four fingers beneath the tightened girth and your horse's hide. Be careful not to strangle her, but be sure that your saddle won't slide off as soon as you set your foot in the stirrup. Some horses like to take a deep breath at the sight of a girth and wait until you mount to let it out. If you are not careful, you may suddenly find yourself plunging sideways around your horse's belly. If your horse uses this trick, try walking or trotting her around for a few minutes before tightening the saddle all the way. The exercise will get her heart rate up and make it harder for her to hold her breath. When she exhales, tighten the girth. When the saddle is secure, walk around to your horse's off side, touching her so she knows where you are, and let down the off stirrup.

The Bridle

In order to bridle your horse, you must remove her halter, which is the strap you placed over her head to lead her around. It is important to hold up the bridle first, disentangle it, and prepare to slip it as swiftly and smoothly as possible over your horse's head. If you do this skillfully, she will appreciate your sureness and gain confidence in you.

Stand on your horse's near side with the bridle in one hand, neatly suspended from the brow and ear pieces. Unbuckle her halter and slide it off. Hold the bit of the bridle on the palm of your flat hand (to avoid getting your fingers nipped) and

offer it to your horse's mouth while guiding the ear piece up behind her ears. If she takes the bit, slide the ear piece behind her ears, buckle the nose strap, and then buckle the throat strap. If she refuses the bit, you may be able to encourage her to open her

Correct placement of the bridle gives your horse confidence in you.

mouth by gently pressing your thumb into the corner of her lips back behind her teeth. When the bridle is fastened, the reins, hanging in front from either side of the bit, will serve as a lead rope.

Dressing to Ride

Now that your horse is tacked and ready to go, make sure that you are as well. First, you must have a helmet. Riding can be dangerous. It is impossible to predict when a sudden scare may cause even the gentlest horse to buck and throw you, or when you might be accidentally kicked or knocked against a fence.

English riders wear black velvet hard hats or black plastic helmets with wide chin straps and small brims. Western riders have historically worn straw or felt cowboy hats that offered no protection against a fall. Today, riding stores sell helmets that fit inside straw or felt cowboy hats, allowing you to keep the Western look while staying safe.

You may want to wear gloves. Your horse is much stronger than you are and controlling her with leather reins or a lead rope may cause blisters or rope burns. You also need pants that allow you to move but that are not

This English rider and his Appaloosa are looking good after doing well in a show.

Western-style rider

baggy. English riders tend to wear jodhpurs or breeches of snug stretch fabrics. Western riders often wear leather chaps over that most American piece of useful clothing: blue jeans.

You will need boots to give you control in the saddle and to protect your feet if your horse accidentally steps on you. Never wear sandals, and never, ever go barefoot around horses. Getting your foot stepped on (and yes, it DOES happen) hurts bad enough in sturdy, protective shoes. Bare feet can be seriously injured by a horse's hoof. English riders generally wear knee-high rubber or leather boots with breeches or short, lace-up jodhpur boots. Western riders favor the cowboy boot.

Choose something strong but not too thick, and be careful to avoid soles with heavy traction such as hiking boots. A chunky sole is more likely to get caught in your stirrups, whereas a smooth-soled boot will move in and out of the stirrups more easily. This is much safer should you need to dismount in a hurry!

If you plan to ride in extreme heat or cold or in strong sunlight, dress accordingly. In the summer, wear light clothing that will not get hot in the sun. Choose loose cotton shirts, cotton breeches or jeans, sunglasses, and lots of sunblock. In the winter, wear layers of warm natural fibers like wool, or toasty synthetics like polyester fleece. If you find yourself too hot at midday, you can peel off a jacket or sweater, and then put it back on as the temperature drops toward evening.

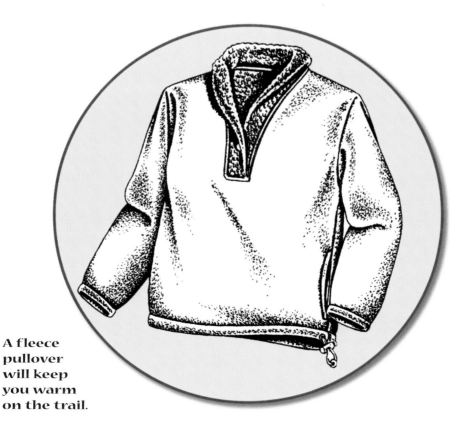

A fleece pullover will keep you warm on the trail.

5 Learning to Ride

Learn to mount your horse with confidence.

When your horse is properly tacked up and you are properly dressed, lead her into the open space of the stable yard. In order to mount, stand on her near side and lift the reins back over her head. Hold the reins in your left hand and rest it on the pommel. Place your other hand on the cantle. Lift your left foot into the stirrup and push yourself into a standing position. Swing your right foot over the horse's hindquarters, being careful not to kick her. Sit down gently on top of your horse. Feel around for the other stirrup with your right foot. Now check the lengths of both stirrups. When you feel secure in your adjustments, sit up straight. Keep your heels down and your hands low and together over your horse's withers. When you want to trot forward, let some slack into the reins and press your heels against your horse's sides.

Before you gallop out of the stable yard and into the sunset, it is important to figure out your skill level. Perhaps you are a beginner and have no experience with horses but have read lots of books and are dying to learn. Perhaps you have taken a few lessons and can walk, stop, turn, and trot. If you have had more than a few lessons, you are confident on a well-behaved horse. If you can walk, trot, and canter comfortably, you are probably an advanced beginner.

By the time you have reached an intermediate level, you will be able to walk, trot, and canter easily. You will be able to perform such basic maneuvers as trotting in circles or serpentines, or trickier maneuvers such as cantering diagonally across a corral, slowing to a trot around one end of the ring, and cantering back along the other diagonal. You may even be able to clear small jumps.

When learning to ride, you must first learn how to feel what your body and the horse's body are doing at different speeds and gaits. Once you understand how a horse moves and how you move with it, you must learn how to use your body to direct the horse's motion. One of the best ways to accustom yourself to the feel of a horse is to ride with your eyes closed. Allow a friend or your instructor to lead your horse, then close your eyes and concentrate on the pattern of your horse's walk. At first, everything will feel strange, but quite soon you will feel improvement in your balance and in your physical reactions to your horse's motion.

A Horse's Gaits

Your horse has four legs. This makes for much more complicated gaits than your own. Think about where each leg is

This horse is moving at a canter.

when your horse walks. Learn to anticipate the rhythm of the four hooves hitting the ground. At a walk, you will have time to feel the separate motion of each leg. As your horse lifts its near hind leg, you will feel the horse's near side lift with it, lifting you and tipping you slightly forward. As the leg lands, you will descend and tilt back on the near side as you rise up on the off side. At a trot, you will feel two strong, staccato beats. At the canter, you will feel three beats: two quick bumps, and a long, muscular lope.

The better your physical understanding of your horse's gaits, the better you will be able to communicate your desires to your horse. You will be able to convey your intentions to

The better you understand your horse physically, the better you will be able to communicate your desires to her.

A horse can read his or her rider's body language.

your horse through physical signals, like pressing your horse's sides with your heels or calves for speed and pulling back on the reins to slow or stop your horse. A horse can also read its rider's body language. A rider who urges a horse to speed up generally leans forward, whereas a rider who wants to stop leans back. It is important not to send mixed signals, like kicking your horse's sides while leaning back and tugging on the reins. As you improve your physical understanding of your horse's motion, your signals and body language will grow more consistent, more effective, and subtler. When you are riding in perfect harmony with your horse, your signals will be invisible to an observer.

A major factor in your ability to ride well and to control your horse is the development of a deep seat. This means sitting deep in the saddle with your back straight, your hands and heels low, your eyes forward, and your muscles alert and relaxed. Your seat is your major point of contact with your horse. If you are steady and firm in the saddle, you will move with your horse and stay put on turns, at high speeds, and over jumps. Your horse will be attuned to your presence and will sense any slight variation as a signal rather than as a random bump from a sack of potatoes.

Your instructor will have suggestions to help you find and improve your seat. Some people find it useful to pull up on the pommel with one hand and the cantle with the other and physically push themselves down into the saddle. Your instructor may also improve your seat by having you ride bareback. In the beginning, riding bareback feels very insecure, but it forces you to find a true sense of balance on your horse's back.

Horses with different types of training learn to respond to different commands from their riders. For the most part, however, there are some near-universal signals that should enable you to ride most schooled horses in the United States. To walk, nudge your horse with your heels or squeeze with your calves. As she starts to move forward, think about the alignment of your body. Keep your back straight, your head up, your eyes and shoulders forward, and your hands and heels down. Keep your legs and torso still and let your hips move with your horse. Imagine that your body grows into your horse's body at the saddle like a centaur.

When you want to speed up to a trot, loosen your reins, lean forward, and press your horse's sides with your legs or heels. The sitting trot is pretty bumpy. Try to absorb the motion and keep your upper body still. English riders, whose saddles are flatter than deep Western saddles, use a posting trot. Posting is an up-and-down motion timed to the bounce of a horse's trot. It allows you to take most of the shock in your flexed legs. Bear in mind that at any speed, it is danger-

The gallop, although frightening at first, can be exhilarating.

ous to allow yourself to bump from side to side because you might bounce off.

To canter, add more pressure with your legs and wait to break out of the bouncy trot into the smooth, long thump of the canter. Keep your body straight, your hands and heels down, and your seat as deep as possible. Do not lean forward. Some horses canter so smoothly that you will feel glued into your saddle as your legs stretch down with the motion of each stride.

Past the canter is the gallop, which, although frightening at first, can be exhilarating. Be sure of your seat and your horse before you attempt to gallop. After the gallop comes the flat-out run, which is mainly appropriate for the racetrack.

Once you are fully comfortable with your horse, you will be able to gallop with confidence and even jump over small streams or low walls. It is important to remember that your horse is a living, intelligent creature with an innate understanding of her world and her own capabilities. Be careful not to push her past her limits or treat her disrespectfully. If you ask your horse to jump a fence that looks higher than anything you've jumped before, or that hides the ground on the far side, or that caps the end of an already long day, and she refuses, she may be thinking more clearly than you are.

6 On the Trail

The pleasures of trail riding are too many to list.

Once you have developed your basic skills—and long before you are galloping or leaping over tall gates—you will be ready to step out onto the trail. The pleasures of trail riding are too many to list. If you love horses and you love nature, there is nothing in the world that can compare with exploring the outdoors with your horse as your companion. Every area of the country has some place set aside for trail riders. There is even horseback riding in some of the parks in New York City.

As always, when you are riding on the

trail, concentrate on your seat. Ride with a loose rein. Allow your environment to help determine your speed and let your horse make footing choices without your guidance or interference. Trail riding often involves climbing and descending, which means that your horse is working harder than usual and needs your cooperation. When heading uphill, keep your weight low and steady. Do not lean on your horse's neck as this can interfere with her balance. To find the correct angle for your body on an incline, align yourself with the vertical trunks of the passing trees. Maintain your deep seat by pushing down in the stirrups. Do not hang onto the saddle as this can add pressure to your horse's girth. If you must, grab her mane; it won't hurt her and it will stabilize you over her center.

Allow your horse to stop and rest when she needs to, and when you stop, turn sideways so that she is not standing at an angle on an incline. Riding uphill can be exhilarating; riding downhill can be terrifying. The full weight of you and your horse create a powerful downward momentum. Your horse's neck will look dangerously far below you. Keep in mind that your horse needs your help to get down the hill safely. Do not panic, tense up, lean back, or sway from side to side. All of these things will interfere with her balance.

When you ride downhill, concentrate on centering your body and steadying your weight for your horse. Stand slightly in your stirrups so that you are barely touching the saddle and are absorbing the bumping with your legs. Keep yourself at the same angle as the passing trees. Help by watching out for particularly bad or slippery footing and lean into the opposite stirrup (on the flank opposite the foreleg that is carrying the weight) to balance her motion.

The Ideal Trail Horse

If your horse is not a seasoned trail rider, build up to serious trail work slowly. Not all horses are born trail riders. Some have trouble keeping their footing in sticky mud or on slippery rocks. If trail riding is your favorite kind of riding, you will want to keep in mind the attributes of the ideal trail horse when you are looking for a horse of your own.

The typical trail horse is extremely surefooted. She combines a long stride, a low-set head, strong bones, and wiry, adaptable muscles. She needs to be agile, intelligent, and brave. She also needs to be capable of making quick, correct decisions when picking through loose stones, navigating slick rocks, or crossing narrow ledges. If you like steep or mountainous terrain, you may prefer a horse with powerful hindquarters and large, steady hooves.

A trail ride can be a very social experience.

If you intend to ride in groups, you will want a horse who does not mind walking before or behind other horses. If you do find yourself on a horse who nips or kicks, you will have to ride alertly and warn anyone who comes near you of the danger. On the trail, your horse may startle easily. The first time you ride outside, your

Views on the trail can be breathtaking.

horse may spook at the sound of pine boughs, the smell of burning leaves, or the sight of a flight of monarch butterflies. Over time, she will grow accustomed to some things and you will learn which others to avoid entirely. It is important to be sensitive to your horse's fears and dislikes. Let her know that

47

Horse Whispering

Sam Powell is a former rodeo cowboy and "horse whisperer" (and inspired a movie with Robert Redford called The Horse Whisperer) who has spent his entire life learning about horses. As a boy, he spent many hours observing horses in the wilds of Arizona and Nevada. He first learned to "break" horses in the traditional style, which resulted in plenty of broken bones for both cowboys and horses. Eventually, Sam began to question the need to break horses so violently. He has developed a new method of horse training called Teaching by Asking. Today he lives near Nashville, Tennessee, and teaches people how to communicate with their horses by learning to read horse body language.

you understand and sympathize even if you have no choice but to pass the smelly rabbit farm down the road or a noisy local airfield.

Horse trainers have different approaches to helping horses learn to handle fear. Some recommend facing down a threat. Some say you should reproduce a disturbance, like the sound of a lawn mower, until it ceases to alarm your horse. Still others maintain that you should teach your horse how to ignore what you, the rider, tell her to ignore. All of these methods involve teaching your horse that the unknown is not always scary. They also stress the importance of teaching a horse to trust a rider.

Teaching a horse to behave calmly is important because an easily spooked horse poses a danger to itself, its rider, and anyone else nearby. A horse that rears or bolts can throw you or trample another animal or person. As always, it is imperative to develop a strong seat in order to hang on and exert your calm, sensible will over your panicking horse. You must always reassure your horse, and yourself, that you are in control.

7 The Dangers of Trail Riding

Trail riding can be exhausting and unpredictable. It can also be dangerous. Whether you plan a quick half-day trot around the neighborhood or a week-long trek into the desert, it is important to be prepared physically and psychologically for what might go wrong. When you are first learning to ride, you will be tired and sore in parts of your body you never thought could get

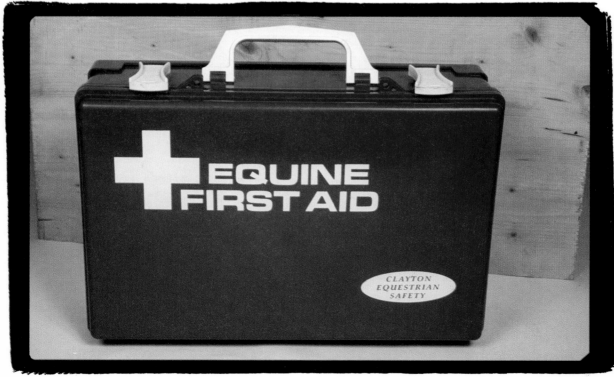

Your horse may need first aid.

sore; namely your rear and the insides of your legs! If you push yourself too hard, you may strain a muscle or tendon or sprain a ligament. It is important to learn some basic first-aid rules (such as RICE: Rest, Ice, Compression, and Elevation for strains and sprains) and to make a point of carrying bandages and antibiotic ointment for minor cuts and scrapes.

All outdoor sports put you at risk of sun damage. Always wear a riding helmet with a brim, as well as sunglasses and sunblock on days when there is any danger of sunburn. In addition, be aware that heat stress can lead to fatigue, exhaustion, errors in judgment, and eventually heatstroke. On a hot day, a serious ride may drain you of a gallon of fluid every hour. Minor heat stress can cause headaches, a quickened pulse, and fatigue. If you feel any of these symptoms, rest in the shade and drink water until you feel normal. More serious heat stress will make you pale, sweaty, weak, and nauseated. Severe heat stress can trigger heatstroke. Victims of severe heat stress look hot and flushed. Their temperatures rise, they breathe rapidly, and they stop sweating. They need immediate medical help.

Heat is not the only outdoor danger. Cold or damp weather can interfere with your circulation. In extreme

A canteen

circumstances, it can cause frostbite. In a sudden snow or rainstorm, you may run the risk of hypothermia, a state in which your body temperature drops to dangerous levels. Hypothermia is made worse by hunger and fatigue and needs to be treated by a doctor.

The air at high mountain altitudes is thinner than air at sea level. This means that it provides less oxygen to you and your horse. This can make you feel dizzy and weak. It can also affect your judgment. If you plan a trail riding trip in higher or more mountainous terrain than where you and your horse live, make sure that you take a day or two for both of your systems to adjust to the higher altitude before you undertake any strenuous riding.

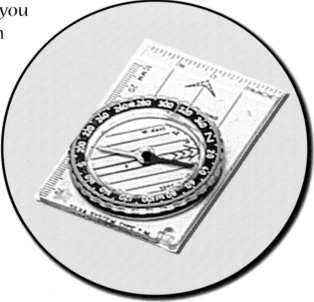

A simple compass

8 Competitive Trail Riding

Dressed for show

Riding for pleasure may whet your appetite for greater challenges in competitive riding. Two of the oldest horse sports are hunting (today this usually means fox hunting and does not involve the death of the fox) and polo, which is about two thousand years old. Polo is a grueling and dangerous sport. It demands incredible speed and precision from its "polo ponies." Similarly, Thoroughbred racing is very much about breeding and is pretty much restricted to professional athletes.

Showing and competition by amateurs, from the local to national level, has only existed since the late nineteenth century. English showing has its roots in fox hunting and military schooling. It includes jumping, dressage (performing precision movements), and halter show classes in which horses are judged by breed and appearance. Western events derive from cattle ranching. Competition here includes rodeo work, lassoing, and barrel racing to test a horse's quickness and coordination.

Competitive Trail Riding

If you love spending time in the wilderness and also want the challenge of competition, you should explore competitive trail riding. Competitive distance riding consists of organized distance rides in which your goal is to cover ground more efficiently than your competitors. Much as runners prepare for months or years to run marathons, you will need to spend months conditioning your horse to improve her endurance. Some distance rides are only a few miles; others are hundreds of miles long and involve varied and unpredictable terrain. Distance riding is probably the greatest test of horse-and-rider cooperation.

In order to train for a distance event, you will need to find terrain similar to that of the course. You will want to consider mud and water conditions, rocky or treacherous surfaces, and steepness. You will also want to think about the possibility of rain or bad weather, and of extreme cold and heat. You will need to start riding comparable distances in order to learn to pace yourself. You also need to learn how to pace your horse. This involves figuring out how much rest and water she needs at different temperatures and on different types of terrain. Most distance riding is performed at the efficient trot, which can cover ground

Sitting for hours on a trotting horse can be grueling.

at ten to twelve miles per hour without straining your horse. Riders beware! Sitting on a trotting horse for hours at a time can be a grueling, bumpy ride for those who are not used to it. For tricky or treacherous stretches, slow to a walk.

     Competitive trail riding blends pleasure riding with serious horsemanship. It offers the scenery and companionship of the trail ride and demands an in-depth knowledge of trail riding skills as well as of horse health, horse physiology, and horse psychology. Competitive trail riding is also serious because of its length. Where a show jumper

Trail riding demands high levels of communication, sympathy, and loyalty between horse and rider.

may complete a course in ten minutes, a distance rider may be on the trail for ten days. Trail riding is not about teaching your horse a particular skill and honing that skill for a short performance in the ring. Rather, it is a comprehensive horse-back riding experience. It encompasses every element of good riding and demands high levels of communication, sympathy, and loyalty between horse and rider. When you are finally able to take your horse out on the trail for a long ride, you will experience a unique sense of accomplishment that few other recreational activities can provide.

Glossary

Appaloosa
A breed of horse distinguishable by its spotted coat. The Appaloosa is an American breed.

Arabian
An ancient North African breed of horse distinguishable by its conformation, its stamina, its intelligence, and its spirited temperament.

Dished face
A phrase used to describe a feature of a horse's conformation in which the profile of the face looks slightly concave; usually a sign of Arabian breeding.

Dressage
A style of competitive riding that emphasizes precision maneuvers and control of the horse by imperceptible commands.

Foal
A baby horse less than one year old.

Frog
The triangle of sensitive flesh in a horse's hoof.

Hand
A length of four inches. A horse's height is measured in hands from the ground up to the shoulder.

Herd

A community of grazing animals, such as horses or cows. Herd animals are
social in nature and tend to be easily guided by a dominant member of
the herd or a human master.

Interbreeding

Mating two different breeds of horses to produce a foal with the traits of
both parents.

Paint

A breed of horse distinguishable by its splotchy coat that
resembles a paint-splattered surface. The Paint is an American breed.

Palomino

A breed of horse distinguishable by its tawny golden body and white mane
and tail. The Palomino is an American breed.

Seat

How a rider sits in the saddle. A secure seat is the mark of a capable rider.

Spook

To startle a horse with a loud noise or sudden movement.

Stallion

An ungelded male horse. Stallions are usually larger, more muscular, and
higher spirited than mares or geldings of the same breed. Only experienced riders and handlers should work with stallions.

Surefooted

The ability to travel smoothly and safely on rocky, slippery, or difficult terrain.

Tack

Riding gear worn by horses, such as saddles and bridles.

Resources

Youth Show and Contest Associations

Intercollegiate Horse Show Association
P. O. Box 741
Stony Brook, NY 11790-0741
(516) 751-2803

National 4-H Council
7100 Connecticut Avenue
Chevy Chase, MD 20815

National Future Farmers of America Foundation
P.O. Box 45205
Madison, WI 53744-5205
(608) 829-3105

National High School Rodeo Association, Inc.
11178 North Huron, Suite 7
Denver, CO 80234
(303) 452-0820

National Little Britches Rodeo Association
1045 West Rio Grande
Colorado Springs, CO 80906
(719) 389-0333

Other Resources

American Horse Council
1700 K Street NW, Suite 300
Washington, DC 20006

American Riding Instructor Certification Program
P. O. Box 282
Alton Bay, NH 03810

Horsemanship Safety Association
P.O. Drawer 39
Fentress, TX 79622

United States Pony Club
4071 Iron Works Pike
Lexington, KY 40511

For Further Reading

Hill, Cherry. *Making Not Breaking*. Ossining, NY: Breakthrough
   Publications, 1992.

Kirksmith, Tommie. *Western Performance: A Guide for Young Riders*. New
   York: Howell Book House, 1993.

Loomis, Bob. *Reining: The Art of Performance in Horses*. Austin, TX:
   EquiMedia, 1990.

McBane, Susan, and Helen Douglas-Cooper. *Horse Facts*. New York:
   Barnes & Noble, 1998.

Strickland, Charlene. *Western Riding*. Pownal, VT: Storey
   Communications, 1995.

Magazines

California Horse Review
P.O. Box 1238
Rancho Cordova, CA 95741

Horse & Rider
12265 West Bayand, Suite 300
Lakewood, CO 80228

Practical Horseman
P.O. Box 589
Unionville, PA 19375

Western Horseman
P. O. Box 7980
 Colorado Springs, CO 80933

Index

Credits

About the Author

Alison Stark Draper is a writer and editor. She lives in New York City and the Catskills.

Photo Credits

Cover photo © John Eastcott/VVA Momatiuk/Image Works; p. 5, 30, 32, 36, 39, 40 & 56 by B. Van Lindt; p. 6 © Archive Photo; p. 8 © Gianni Dagli Orti/Corbis; p. 9 © Mark Newman/ International Stock; p. 11 © Archive Photo; p. 12 © Ron Maratea/ International Stock; p. 15 © Mark Newman/International Stock; p. 16 © Kit Houghton/Corbis; p. 17 © Peter Krinninger/ International Stock; p. 19 © Norris Clark/International Stock; p. 20 © Kit Houghton/Corbis; p. 22 © Black Stallion Returns/Everett Collection, Inc.; p. 23 © Buzz Binzen/International Stock; p. 26 © Frederick Lewis/Archive Photo; p. 27 © Kit Houghton/Corbis; p. 28 © Uli Degwert/International Stock; p. 29 © Morton Beebe/Corbis; p. 33 © Kit Houghton/Corbis; p. 34 © Lowell Georgia/Corbis; p. 38 © Kit Houghton/Corbis; p. 42 © Diana Cook/Uniphoto; p. 44 © John Plummer/Uniphoto; p. 46 © Daemmrich/ The Image Works; p. 47 © Caroline Wood/Uniphoto; p. 48 © The Horse Whisperer/Everett Collection; p. 50 © Kit Houghton/Corbis; p. 52 by Scott Bauer; p. 53 © Philip Gould/Corbis; p. 55 © Hughes Photography.

Photos on cover and pages 5, 30, 32, 36, 39, 40 & 56 made possible with the cooperation of Dixie Dew Riding Stables, Forest Hills, NY.

Series Design

Oliver H. Rosenberg

Layout

Law Alsobrook